CHOOSE TO CHANGE

CHOOSE TO CHANGE

Unverified perception that shapes or determines our behavioural patterns, are a people destroyer phenomena which robs us all of fulfilled lives we have been destined to experience, thus keeping us in bondage.

Franklin Jones Visser

Rev. date: 04/22/2014

To order additional copies of this book, contact:
Xlibris Corporation
0-800-644-6988
www.xlibrispublishing.co.uk
Orders@xlibrispublishing.co.uk
516120

Contents

1. Foreword 7

2. Introduction 9

3. Chapter 1   A Man in the Street Perspective 11

4. Chapter 2   Product of Our Upbringing 13

5. Chapter 3   Lack of Effective Communication 15

6. Chapter 4   Self-image 18

7. Chapter 5   Conflict Resolution 21

8. Chapter 6   What Goes Around Comes Around 24

9. Chapter 7   What Makes People Tick 27

10. Chapter 8   Values, Principles and Beliefs 29

11. Chapter 9   You Are What You Digest 31

12. Chapter 10   Be Real 33

13. Chapter 11   Leadership 35

14. Chapter 12   Work At Your Dreams 38

15. Chapter 13   It's Never Too Late 40

16. Chapter 14   Men Pleaser Or God Pleaser 42

17. Chapter 15   How To Treat Others 44

18. Chapter 16   Social, Economic and Political Influences 47

19. Conclusion 53

Foreword

Change is constant and whether we choose not to change, we will be impacted by the realities thereof. Given the era of technological advancement and knowledge, resistance to change will be suicidal and will keeping us in darkness and limiting us in becoming the real us, in terms of our God-given potential.

We must never underestimate the power of conditioning that to a main extend forms our behaviour in general, which can help us in replacing bad behaviour with more accepted behaviour based on our values, beliefs and principles. The good news is we all can change if we willingly choose to change to the best and so transforming our society at large, by embracing change personally. The current reality is that we must reconstruct our lives in a manner that integrates the good and solid values and traditions of all of our upbringing, instead of just throwing it away in the pursue of just "doing it our ways". Our upbringing does not in any way indicate or determine our ability to achieve in live with regards to our individual dreams, but rather serves as a reference point from where we can excel in taking ownership of our destiny and purpose in life. This can only realized by personal realistic goal setting, thus paving the way step by step in achieving our objectives(page 7).

Were we are at is in most instances the result of our yesterday that is past tense. We go through life not necessarily conscious of the manner in how we project or sell ourselves to the outside world on the one hand, and the response of the outside world on the other hand. Bottom line we need to challenge ourselves, "Am I happy with were I am?" "How did I arrived here?" "Were do I want to be?" "What do I desire from the bottom of my heart?" "What is my strength and that I am enjoying the most?" "How do I get from were I am to were I want to be?". There is a tendency that we want to change others and everything and everyone but fail to see that it begins with us! Either we choose to change and becoming what God predestined us to become in union with Christ Jesus, or we become products of all shorts of influences of our time and age.

Every new day offers something new! Today we have to prove to ourselves what we have learned of the total of our yesterdays. Change is inevitable and when we choose to change not for the sake to change, but to what extend we can leave this life a better place by contributing constructively through concerted effort. We have to channel our energies in pursuing our dreams by setting realistic personal goals.

We are living in a world of constant change and whenever we resist change in principle we choose to become stagnant and are doomed to become outdated and irrelevant, and ourselves and others are not living up to our full potential. My prayer is that we all will change our minds and be renewed! Acts 3:19 says "*(Change your mind)—Repent, then, and turn to God, so that your sins may be wiped out, that times of refreshing may come from the Lord,*" However, how we think about ourselves will ultimately determines how we perceive others to be and does at the end influence the way we responsibly handle perceptions of others. You are who you think you are.

Proverbs 23:7 says "*For as he thinks in his heart, so is he . . .*" (Amp. & NKJV) (page 10)

Introduction

Did you ever find yourselves in conversations with people unexpectedly and sometimes unprepared and hear a person making statements, which reflects that you were the topic of discussion or they just make known what they think about your life in general. It is in actual fact amazing that people do not put an effort to protect themselves from self exposure. We walking around with preconceived ideas and prejudge mental approaches towards others and wonder why we lack fulfilment in relationships in general. We associate ourselves with like minded people who enjoy talking about others in inappropriate manner. Surely it is common the practise of gossiping amongst people who lack depth and integrity, without realizing that they limit themselves and putting themselves in bondage. Even peoples attitudes tell it all, but we must be caution not to easily jump to conclusions or assumptions. Our attitude towards others can make or break us! One thing is for sure that our behaviour does give us away. Our body languages, tone of voices, facial expressions do at times give others the impression of how we value and think about them.

I believe still that people are the most important asset on this planet earth. Regardless of the high technological area, we are in a great need for high touch. We ought to take care of society by taking care of those crossing our paths, even if it is only by a positive attitude we shows towards people. Considering all negative statistics across our globe like the crime rate, war, terrorism, rape, theft, corruption, divorce rate, abortion rate, unemployment rate, HIV and AIDS rate, etc we have not yet learned how to talk to one another in a manner that will produce the opposite effect. We choose rather to be part of the problems instead of being part of the solutions. We need to come out of our closets and be real for a change and confront the obvious in order that the truth can be prevailing. A discipline approach in interacting with the people in our world will help us in establishing the truth, and set us free from all possible misperceptions. I believe if we think right, we can talk right and only then we can live right. We need to process methodically our perceptions through ensuring the verification of all perceptions from where we alter our behaviour to a large extend towards people in general.

For us to achieve different results we ought to do things differently, and herewith accept the reality, the willingness to change and to adopt the required discipline necessary to be applied. We must choose to change or remain at the known and settles with unfulfilled relationships or unresolved issues, which occupies unnecessary brain capacity and waste of time. We need to get out from our various comfort zones and venture out in setting and pursuing realistic goals in order to develop to our full potential. The saying is so true: "if you fail to plan you plan to fail" emphasising that you will not achieve anything which you didn't set your mind upon.

Chapter 1

A Man in the Street Perspective

Real life occurs when people, for various reasons, in various places and at various times interact with one another. I'm an ordinary person trying to speak for thousands and maybe millions of people who are silent, and only observe the world from their own individual world perspective with their own respective frame of reference. My background in approaching this vital people destroyer phenomenon namely, unverified perceptions and the necessity to change, which results mostly in negative behaviour, stems from my personal walk with God for the past 29 years. As a disciple of Christ I endeavour to put some light on defects in our general behavioural patterns that hampers or hinders our relationship with one another, and consequently robs ourselves of tremendous relationship and general life fulfilment.

I believe that a person is as rich as he is in his relationship with others. The Church's greatest challenge lies in the ability to demonstrate the love of God in relation to people. Many Christians live in a world of their own by only focussing on a self entertained spirituality which for some or other reason only benefits them at the cost of sharing themselves with others in the body of Christ or to the world they live in. I have come across many Christians who maintain a so-called strong spiritual life that they ironically evidently lack the ability to engage in ordinary day-to-day conversations with others. Ever heard about the saying: "so heavenly minded and of earthly no good". Strangely, we have unlearned the old basic fundamentals of relationship building and that is the willingness and openness to listen to one another seriously and attentively and the ability to share one self with others you know listens.

I do value relationships in general and firmly believe that one can be known by the kind of friends you have on various levels. Why do people's behaviour change all the time in our dealings with one another. For me the Bible furnishes the ultimate guidelines or parameters on how we ought to behave towards one another and as an appropriate example we can look at the first epistle of John 4:7-21 with specific reference to verse 12: ***"No one has ever seen God; but if we love one another, God lives in us and his love is made complete in us."*** (N.I.V). We must refrain from the mentality of practising a kind of Christianity that suites us without adhering to the requirements or challenges of Scripture. We must adjust to Biblical standards, values and principles and not the other way around. We are commissioned by Christ to love one another in His manner of love displayed to us, as a testimony to the world that we are his disciples (John 13:34-35). Surely the greatest commandment should pause us in our steps of life, emphasizing the importance of love for God to be practised and seen in our relationship towards one another (Mark 12:29-31). Our understanding of God and our interpretation and application of Scripture are reflected in our relationship with all people. So if you really believe in God and living a sacrificial heart-faith relationship, we ought to show it by the way we live our lives. Our lives must be a living epistle or sermon or the only Bible some people would ever read. We must demonstrate our faith of which we are graciously allowed, to live in an active living experiential love relationship with God our Father, and the Lord Jesus Christ, and with the Holy Spirit.

The man in the street at times struggles how to handle this unpredictability of men's changing behaviour which unnecessary robs us all of joy and peace. This change in behaviour causes a breakdown in communication—and consequently relationships—and need to be taken into account and not to be underestimated. If we can manage and respond to this phenomenon better we can contribute to other's self-worth and happiness and we can rise to a higher level of life fulfilment. The key here is to understand others rather than to be understood by them. So our workplaces, family ties and society at large offer a vast opportunity to make our world a better place by treating one another in a more dignified manner. Each person as important as the next!

Chapter 2

Product of Our Upbringing

We tend to defend, protect or justify our misbehaviour by the way we have been brought up. We react to life instantaneously without realising the impact of our behaviour towards others—whether good or bad. For real revolution to occur in our world of relationships we have to analyse the way we generally behave and consciously and critically change the way we think in order to change our behaviour to what is more conducive for human relationships. We must be builders of people in stead of breaking people down and not contributing towards an environment that prevents them to become what God predestined them to become in union with Christ. The Prophet Jeremiah 29:11 said: *"For I know the plans I have for you," declares the Lord, "plans to prosper you and not to harm you, plans to give you hope and a future."* Man in his design and capabilities are an awesome reflection of God and the value the Creator attaches to the crown of his creation (Psalm 8:4 *"What is man that you are mindful of him,* the son of man that you care for him?"*).

In my experience with interacting with people in various workplaces and industries throughout the years I have learned that we create or contribute through our attitude an atmosphere, which in turn determines or influences people's behaviour towards us to a great extend. As a disciple of Christ I experienced through the past 29 years that following Jesus means a journey of continual **change into His likeness—never to be the same again!** Christ can change the way we think about others and consequently change our behaviour towards them. We don't need to stay at the negative ways we have been accumulated throughout the years or being brought up, that degrade or belittle other people and think of ourselves as better than others. We must not even think in turn of ourselves as inferior and insignificant to others. We must not deny the power of our conditioned negative behavioural patterns programmed through the years that limits us and others, thus preventing us in reaching our full potential. Jesus says in John 10:10 "The thief comes only to steal and kill and destroy; *I have come that they may have life, and have it to the full.*" I personally think we do however mess it up in our relationship towards one another in our churches and towards those outside the confines of our church walls, and we need to get back at mastering the fundamental basics of engaging positively in relationships.

We obviously cannot go back into our past and change the way we have been brought up that influences our behaviour negatively, but we can change current identifiable negative behaviour by changing the way we think. Changed behaviour represents an intervention that took place that caused or triggered that change to the benefit of relationships. We must strife towards a scenario of a win-win situation in relationship building. **One amazing reality of knowing and serving Christ is the continual process of Him changing us from the inside-out, never to be the same again!** We don't need to park at our past and put up memorials, but we can undo the past by embracing our future of purpose and destiny as He transforms us more into His likeness. Apostle Paul says in 2 Corinthians 3:18 "And we, who with unveiled faces all reflect the Lord's glory, *are being transformed into his likeness with* ever-increasing glory, which comes from the Lord, who is the Spirit." We all got an equal opportunity to develop our unique potential when we accept our responsibility to die empty in our pursuit of living to the full. We must rather become enslaved in what we can become in and through Him, than to remain products of our upbringing. If we resist change we unfortunately decide on a suicidal approach of maintaining the old us.

We must never underestimate the power of conditioning that to a main extend forms our behaviour in general, which can help us in replacing bad behaviour with more accepted behaviour based on our values, beliefs and principles. The good news is we all can change if we willingly choose to change to the best and so transforming our society at large, by embracing change personally. The current reality is that we must reconstruct our lives in a manner that integrates the good and solid values and traditions of all of our upbringing, instead of just throwing it away in the pursue of just "doing it our ways". Our upbringing does not in any way indicate or determine our ability to achieve in live with regards to our individual dreams, but rather serves as a reference point from where we can excel in taking ownership of our destiny and purpose in life. This can only realized by personal realistic goal setting, thus paving the way step by step in achieving our objectives.

Chapter 3

Lack of Effective Communication

It is humanly impossible to fully discover self to the fullest on a distant-island, isolated approach. No one person can grow on his own. We need to relate, and effectively relate, to people in order to discover and develop to our full potential. Our interactions with others afford us the opportunity to exercise our basic fundamental need as a social being. When we allow our behavioural patterns to be shaped or influenced by poor or ineffective communication, it can be destructive and a destroyer of good relationships. As I said before, when we allow unverified perceptions to determine our behaviour, we are not making progress in fostering mutually beneficial relationships.

Communications are the manner by which we share our perceptions and consequent behaviour, whether verbally or non-verbally. It is a well accepted fact that we in general communicate more on a non-verbal fashion. We lack in most times the ability to communicate what we actually mean. We get away or settle with poor expression of ourselves to others which in turn benefits no one at the end. We ought to say what we mean and say what we want others to understand and illuminates all possible misperceptions in the manner and tone we communicate in general. If we can only learn to speak the truth in love uncompromisingly, acknowledging our individual uniqueness and just celebrate our diversity, we can make this world a better place. Ephesians 3:15 says it all: "*Instead, speaking the truth in love*, we will in all things grow up into Him who is the Head, that is Christ."

We must stop trying to maintain a prejudgemental approach towards other people and rather investing in the process of rebuilding and restoring broken relationships, by disallowing unverified perceptions to negatively influence our behaviour. We must not block the growth of relationships by our negative attitudes in our interaction with people in general. We all tend to park at the known, which at times represents many of our comfort zones and evidently lack the ability to be open and willing to engage in new relationships. With clear, open, honest, respectful communications we can relate to others in a more dignified manner, hence ensuring and creating more fulfilling relationships. All of our unnecessary conflicts amongst one another can be easily resolved if we only pursue on a more clearly specified manner of communication which make little or no room for misinterpretations and minimising all possible misunderstanding. We must excel in precisely formulating our thoughts in communicating with our world and precisely convey to others what we really mean or want them to understand or just in simple words what we want to say or know from them.

One of our day-to-day mistakes in our world of communications is that we lack to grasp the basic dynamics of listening and talking. James 1:19(b)-20 rightfully says *"Everyone should be quick to listen, slow to speak and slow to become angry,* for man's anger does not bring about the righteous life that God desires." Many elderly people I came across said: "You have got two ears to listen more and one mouth to speak less." In our conversations with others we tend most of the time to do the talking, with little interest to really listen to the other party. We can't wait for others to finish talking just to tell our story and at times we display impatience and arrogance by interrupting others in their talking, just to be heard or enforce ourselves upon them. We need to master the technique of effective listening by asking verifying, clarifying and relevant questions arising from what other people may share with us. Only when we see the bigger picture of others, we can be of help whether on a advisory capacity or just our availability and willingness to listen. Proverbs 18:13 says: *"He who answers before listening—that is folly and his shame."* I believe that in the manner we conduct ourselves in communication with our world we expose our identity, values and principles. Other emotions are also triggered in the process like our insecurities, inferiorities, superiorities and our fear of rejection, just to mention some amongst others.

Effective communication is crucial in illuminating misperceptions which results in people moving apart from each other, instead of growing together, in this life school of learning. We also need to be mindful of the saying of the old and wise people, namely, "It is not what you say, but how you say it," with particular reference to the tone of our voices that counts. We need to break all possible abnormal silence by communicating on a continual basis and refrain from possible "mind games" that imprison people instead of liberating them from all possible form of fear for communicating with the outside world. We need to manage all possible identifiable communication barriers in a positive, hence preparing a win-win way forward for building constructive relationships.

Chapter 4

Self-image

I have touched partly in chapter three on this subject, where we all at times compare ourselves with others which results in us considering ourselves to be inferior or superior to others. A poor self-image can cause us easily to misunderstand others and may quickly trigger us to adjust our behaviour negatively at times, due to unverified perceptions about others. I firmly belief that if we think right we can talk right and we then can live right. What does self-image got to do with perceptions you may ask? Without any doubt I believe that the way we perceive our world influences the way we respond to it! Or to put it the other way around: our self-image whether good or poor greatly influences the way we perceive our world.

In my world of living (as a born again believer through the grace of God) I came to an amazing discovery within the church. Christians confuse poor self-image with humility! We are too proud and consequently fleshly or worldly to acknowledge that we do have an identity crisis—low or poor self-image. It is because we have never realised who we are, where we come from and where we are heading. Regardless what the Bible says who we are in Christ we tend to be conditioned and tend to prefer to project the old me and us. I think we have to critically analyse the way our identity has been formed in the first place throughout our childhood and adulthood, and prayerfully and faithfully replace it with Biblical values and principles. What really matters is what God think, say and plan is for our lives. The Bible also says that it is dangerous to think about what others think or say about you.

All of our unresolved issues and unnecessary conflicts surfaces mainly due to the added phenomena of a lack of good self-esteem which negatively influence our judgement in relation to people. We can only imagine what would result with a person with a low self esteem when it comes to handle perceptions correctly, by verifying it first, before altering his or her behaviour accordingly. It is a given fact that people with a low self-image are to a large extend great underperformers and poor achievers with poor or no confidence. My experience with people with a poor self-image is that they tend to take most of the times, in their world of communications, things personally due to the dominant effect and reality of choosing to maintain a poor self-image. One of the mistakes amongst other we all make from time to time is that we compare ourselves with others, maybe to measure and to see how we are doing. I must live my life based on my personal convictions, beliefs, values and principles and stop living in the world of comparisons. This is the only way we can be real and live up to our full potential and become what God has predestined us to be in union with Christ Jesus. We must have a passion for our vision in life and with head up high, trusting God; we must give our best shot in pursuing living our dreams.

The inside me will be projected to the outside world, so even a person thinking of him or her better than other's judgment, would be contaminated in their dealings of perceptions. Bottom line, if you are a negative person you will see negativity around and in everything people say or do. The same applies if you are a positive person you automatically projects positivism. If you say you are not going to make it—you won't make it, period! To be the real you, in other words to be what God wants you to be, are not related to performance, but on the basis how He values you. Our self-image whether good or bad determines in most instances the degree we are prepared to reach or relate to the outside world. I have seen on managerial levels within companies during meetings how individuals personalized issues on the table due to a lack of a sound self-image. They just displays their hidden agendas and are to a great extend obstructive instead of being a team player, promoting the mission of their organisations. Wherever people are this dominant defect (poor self-image) in our make-up causes us to be non-productive and ineffective and constitute a people destroyer phenomenon. We need to come free from all our bondages that is keeping us in captivity and rob us all off the tremendous blessings and fulfilment God intended, us to have in Christ and in one another. That is why love is the fulfilment of the law as it brings no harm to our neighbours but instead edifies one another. Only when we release ourselves from all negative emotional bondages like poor self-image, bitterness, unforgiveness, hatred, jealousy, undealt hurt or pain, comparison or competition with others, rejection, unfair unbased judgement by others, amongst others, we only then can release those trapped in all shorts of bondages. To be true agents of change we need to be free ourselves!

Isaiah spoke prophetically around 700 B.C about the forthcoming yoke/ bondage destroying ministries of Christ in chapter 61:1-3 "The Spirit of the Sovereign Lord is on me, because the Lord has anointed me . . . *to bind up the brokenhearted, to proclaim freedom for the captives and release from darkness for the prisoner, . . . to bestow on them a crown of beauty instead of ashes, the oil of gladness instead of mourning, and a garment of praise instead of a spirit of despair.*" And the good news is that we the Church, the bride of Christ are endowed with His Spirit to perform the work of the ministry advancing the Kingdom of God. Luke announces the impact of the Holy Spirit upon the lives of the believers of Christ Jesus in Acts 1:8 "*But you will receive power when the Holy Spirit comes on you;* and you will be my witnesses in Jerusalem, and in all Judea and Samaria, and to the ends of the earth." Jesus wrapped it up in His job description of His bride, thus explaining the purpose of the empowerment by the Holy Spirit in Matthew 28:19-20 "*Therefore go and make disciples of all nations, baptizing them in the name of the Father and of the Son and of the Holy Spirit and teaching them to obey everything I have commanded you.* And surely I am with you always, to the very end of the age."

We are living in a world of constant change and whenever we resist change in principle we choose to become stagnant and are doomed to become outdated and irrelevant, and ourselves and others are not living up to our full potential. My prayer is that we all will change our minds and be renewed! Acts 3:19 says "*(Change your mind)—Repent, then, and turn to God, so that your sins may be wiped out, that times of refreshing may come from the Lord,*" However, how we think about ourselves will ultimately determines how we perceive others to be and does at the end influence the way we responsibly handle perceptions of others. You are who you think you are.

Proverbs 23:7 says "*For as he thinks in his heart, so is he . . .*" (Amp. & NKJV)

Chapter 5

Conflict Resolution

Perceptions are inherent part of our daily living and we need to know how to manage it effectively in a manner that, incorrect and unverified one's causes less damage. We do not have control over all things that happens to us, but we can control and determine or choose the way we respond to it. Conflict must not always be seen as negative but rather as an opportunity to put things in perspective and to grow closer to one another. We must celebrate our diversity and uniqueness and acknowledge it in our dealings with one another in all levels of society. An important element in conflict resolution is the ability to separate the issues from people and resolve the matter at hand. We must develop our ability to resolve our differences on a win-win basis.

We all manage conflict differently. Some move in a silent mode and withdraw, hoping the conflict to cease automatically over a period of time. Others respond in a defensive manner and others just personalized matters and acting emotional and irrational. However, I do believe that conflict does afford us all the opportunity to enforce all of our resources and experiences we all accumulated over the years in resolving any conflict at hand on a win-win basis. Problems must be resolve at the core of its origin with all role players involved. All solutions lie within all problems. We need to unpack our conflicts/problems in order to identify it and determine the best remedies possibly available. We at times complicate things unnecessary by making the problem so big and difficult, even to the extend that it intimidates us, that it left us lame and powerless, unable to do anything in order to resolve the matter at hand.

To ignore conflict on the one hand, or to engage in discussions with irrelevant parties on the other hand does not resolve any issue but can only bring harm to the situation. I have learned out of my own mistakes in relationships with people, that to discuss a matter with people (unless it is for advice or consultation) that got nothing to do with the actual conflict situation does only bring harm to the situation at hand. We need to usher ourselves into a culture, in our relationship with people without compromising, to truthfully communicate our values, principles and beliefs without fear. As I said before, Ephesians 3:15 say it all: *"Instead, speaking the truth in love, we will in all things grow up into Him who is the Head, which is Christ."*

The Body of Christ are advised to settles their differences amongst themselves, instead of raising lawsuits against each other and to be judged by unbelievers. 1 Corinthians 6:1 says: *"If any of you has a dispute with another,* dare he take it before the ungodly for judgment instead of before the saints?" Any disputes to be resolved amongst the believers considering their future reality to judge the world. 1 Corinthians 6:2-3 says: "Do you not know that the saints will judge the world? And if *you are to judge the world, are you not competent to judge trivial cases*? Do you not know that we will judge angels? How much more the things of this life!"

Apostle Paul attributed the Corinthians division in the church to the fact that they were still very much worldly, which explained their jealousy and quarrelling amongst each other (1 Corinthians 3:3 "You are still worldly. *For since there is jealousy and quarrelling among you, are you not worldly? Are you not acting like mere man?"*). He further appealed to them in 1 Corinthians 1:10 to agree with one another in order to prevent disunity "I appeal to you, brothers, in the name of our Lord Jesus Christ, that all of you *agree with one another so that there may be no divisions among you and that you may be perfectly united in mind and thought"*.

My experience in General Human Resource Management amongst other disciplines, I do understand that there must be conflict resolution mechanisms within all workplaces to appropriately channel all possible employment related conflicts. However, I came to discover that there are basic fundamental uncompromising principles to be adhered to in order to ensure a safe environment for any conflict resolution. In many a time we lack the guts to confront and hence attempt to resolve the conflicts in our lives. In our modern age of technological advancement that sustaining and promoting our excess to the wealth of information to our disposal, we got all the reason in the world to approach our differences and disagreements, from a more informed angle to produce a win-win result. Ideally it will benefit humanity greatly if we can filter down this win approach in conflict resolution to early childhood and primary school level for all learners. This would eventually lead children to become more aware of their environment, people, their opinions, values and principles.

One golden rule I believe that if you may have a conflict or problem with somebody that you need to go in private to see that person. It is important to address and focus on the issue; what that person did or said that make you unhappy and to refrain from attacking or degrading or discredit the person. We need to separate the matter from the person and go factual through the occurrences that created the negative emotions within us. It is important to truthfully and honestly conveying the identified emotions to the relevant person and grasps the opportunity to verify your perception before believing and adjusting your behaviour negatively towards that particular person. Part of verifying our perceptions are that we need to be open and bighearted in allowing the other party to give explanations, clarifications or just his or her response to our observations or perceptions, thus affording them the *"benefit of the doubt"*. The possibility exists that the other party may choose not to participate wholeheartedly thus preventing real reconciliation or restoration of relationships to occur. Following this root establish the way forward in our relationship with people and are really a worthwhile exercise, as it affords us all the opportunity to put things in perspective and sets the path how future conflicts are to be dealt.

Chapter 6

What Goes Around Comes Around

We all can choose what role to play whether building good or bad relationships; through building or breaking down people. We in most times do not realize that we all do this to a greater or lesser degree by the way we behave ourselves towards those in our world of contact. As I also said before we do not have control over things that happens to us, but we can determine how we want to respond to the things that are happening to us on a day-to-day basis. We can decide to be victors instead of victims of bad behaviour and conduct of other people. We do have all a common responsibility to respond in a positive, meaningful and constructive way in all times as part of our contribution towards society in creating a better life for all. I do firmly believe that this manner of stance with regards to engaging in a more fulfilled manner is empowering and hence contributing towards a culture of making winners of all.

The reality however is that it is easy said than done, as we all are on different levels in our walk with our fellow men and in terms of ourselves. We need to remind ourselves of the reality that the individual's complexity increases within a group situation. The various given personality and character differences together with our various mindsets and conditioned conduct of behaviour, amongst other, are just some of the dynamics that contributing towards the challenge in fostering mutually beneficial relationships. I belief that relationships in general does not grow automatically, but requires all parties involve to work on it through active participation in one way or another. Through our attitudes and behaviour, we are releasing various signals to the outside world, which in turn gets interpreted and activates accordingly all kinds of reactions. To get the desired feedback or results we anticipate, we need to asses the manner we market and sell ourselves and do the necessary adjustment to illuminates all possible unwanted behaviour due to all possible misperceptions or misunderstandings.

The Bible says that life and death lies at the power of the tongue. Proverbs 18:21 "*The tongue has the power of life and death, and those who love it will eat its fruit.*" Ever heard about the saying: what you put in is what you gonna get out or your output reflecting your input or things will backfire? I am reminded about what Scripture says in Luke 6:31 "*Do to others as you would have them do to you*" and in 2 Corinthians 9:6 which interpreted in its context means what *you sow you will reap.* We are making constant choices daily on how we sell, market or projecting ourselves to the outside world. We choose daily on how to respond daily to our world that influences or intimidates us. I belief without the shadow of a doubt that we hurt and build people through our words and attitudes we displays on a daily basis towards them. So we are making enemies and friends daily without realizing the consequences thereof that generates curses instead of Gods blessings upon our lives. We are short-sighted if we think we can get away in ill treating people, who all in turn are according to Genesis 1:26-31, created in the image of God to rule and reign on earth. Categorically no! What goes around comes around!

Apostle James is very clear in chapter 3:6, 9-12 "*The tongue also is a fire,* a world of evil among the parts of the body. It corrupts the whole person, sets the whole course of his life on fire, and is itself set on fire by hell. 9 *With the tongue we praise our Lord and Father, and with it we curse men, who have been made in God's likeness.* 10 Out of the same mouth come praise and cursing. My brothers, this should not be. 11 Can both fresh water and salt water flow from the same spring? 12 My brothers, can a fig tree bear olives, or a grapevine bear figs? Neither can a salt spring produce fresh water." The world we all live in were instituted and are currently since its origin, sustain by an All Knowing, Ever Present and All Mighty God.

God is a just God, on whose principles this world were founded and established. He created the world and establishes universal principles that are unchangeable and we need to be aware thereof and responsibly integrate it in our lifestyles in order to be fruitful and generally blessed. We cannot say, think or act towards people as we wish and treat them in a unworthy or indecent manner and think there are no consequences, and that we will get away with it! No, no, no we will reap what we show. Our wealth and health will be directly negatively impacted when we discriminate against our fellowman as somebody lesser that ourselves. We cannot afford to belittle other people if we realise the consequences thereof. Self examination in our relation to others and God key in ensuring good health and wealth. Apostle Paul instructs believers in Holy Communion to properly examine self before participating, to prevent any unworthy conduct and consequent judgement. Lack thereof he says results in 1 Corinthians 11:30 *"That is why many among you are weak and sick, and a number of you have fallen asleep."*

We must evaluate and assess our motives in dealing with people in general. Honesty, integrity, transparency, truthfulness and faithfulness must safeguard us. Hypocrisy, corruption and fraud must not find as in any way guilty. Galatians 5: 19-21 says: "The acts of the sinful nature are obvious: sexual immorality, impurity and debauchery; 20 idolatry and witchcraft; hatred, discord, jealousy, fits of rage, selfish ambition, dissensions, factions 21 and envy; drunkenness, orgies, and the like. I warn you, as I did before, that those who live like this will not inherit the kingdom of God." In the light of the sinful nature that contradicts or opposes the values of God and as a result prevent us of inheriting the kingdom of God, the Apostle Paul advices us to live a life in the Spirit of God according to Galatians 5: 16 "So I say, *live by the Spirit and you will not gratify the desires of the sinful nature."* In Romans 8:14 Paul emphasised the important criteria that qualifies us in being children of God: "because *those who are led by the Spirit of God are sons of God."*

The cycle of destroying lives by breaking people down through constant negative behaviour must stop if we want to leave this world in a better state, and hence create a better environment more conducive for people to engage with one another thus celebrating our freedom in Christ as affirmed according to Galatians 5:1 *"It is for freedom that Christ has set us free."* Our conduct of behaviour whether good or bad does implicate others and ourselves and we need to be aware thereof, and be accountable for it.

Chapter 7

What Makes People Tick

Thus far we have come to realise again that we are impacting people's lives by our mere thoughts, words and deeds. It is clear that we at some instances are guilty in adjusting our behaviour negatively towards others, based on hear say or just our observations. Understanding the dynamics involve in general communications, we fully grasp the importance in verifying perceptions with all relevant parties to build or justify our consequent behaviour towards people. We need to understand that in reality we will come across people that we don't naturally or automatically click with. Those with whom we just don't "jell" with, we tend to distant ourselves from. Others with whom we just click do not guaranteeing fruitful lasting relationships. We need to accept it as a golden required skill, vital for building effective lasting relationship, that we got to work at it at all times.

As part of our DNA we are selfish in nature only looking to our own interest and wellbeing. That explains in most instances the kind of relationship we have with people, with specific reference to the kind of problems within these relationships that we may experience. Our egos are just too dominant that we are constantly trying to be the centre of attraction and our world revolves around ourselves, what we can get out to gratify the self—what's there in for me that what it appears to be! Apostle Paul wrote to the Philippians Church in chapter 2:3 *"Do nothing out of selfish ambition or vain conceit, but in humility consider others better than yourselves."* Others interest and wellbeing is not of importance to us and we need to get out of our various little worlds and see in what way or another we can contribute towards others wellbeing in fulfilling their dreams and desires. Philippians 2:4 says: *"Each of you should look not only to your own interest, but also to the interests of others.*" Only in adding value to the lives of others we can live meaningful lives which are a far better method of getting our needs and desires met. It is by helping others that we simultaneously investing in the current and future provision of our own needs and desires. It is about sowing and reaping in the kingdom of God what counts, which will guarantee supplied harvest. Our harvest follows our seed and we must never become tired of giving to others. The Bible says in 1 John 3:18 "Dear children, **let us not love with words or tongue but with actions and in truth.**"

I discovered in my experience with people a very powerful denominator in starting to build sound, balance and healthy relationships is to find out what make the other person tick. What is the reference or departing point of really reaching out to others in a manner that motivates them to indeed want to engage with us. This principle when applied work even with the strangest kind of people that crosses our path. To show interest in the real life stories of people afford them the opportunity to take us in their journey of life and even touching their personal world with their permission. To allow people to draw their lives in our presence provide us with valuable personal data of their lives, for us to be informed and to respond to them in a more sensitive and sensible way. People's field of interest, their hobbies, dreams, frustrations, weaknesses, failures, successes amongst others, are important to all of us and we need to have the feedback from people that they respect and appreciates it all, thus approving of who we are. We can with great objectivity propose various options in our counsel or advice to them whenever requested due to all possible unforeseen circumstances. Allowing people to share themselves with us really informs us, with regards to what makes them tick for which we need to be aware of, that can definitely help us to be relevant in our relationship towards them. Surely this is a process and does not happen overnight and requires a lot of patience in our endeavours to surround us with quality fulfilled relationships. I am however still convince that we need to make our friendliness applicable to all we come across, but be selective with those we become close friends with.

Chapter 8

Values, Principles and Beliefs

Our living out are surely a reflection of who we really are on the inside. I believe without any doubt that our behaviour is directly linked with our personal values, principles and belief system. The Bible says that there are nothing that enters a man that make him unclean but that which cometh out of his mouth (Matthew 15:18)! Verses 19-20 continues to share further light *"For out of the heart come evil thoughts, murder, adultery, sexual immorality, theft, false testimony, slander. These are what make a man unclean . . ."* We experience in our day and age a worldwide tendency of immorality and unbiblical laws for example on abortion, prostitution, gambling, and homosexuality amongst others that are destroying humanity. We are living in a fallen world and as sinners are under the control of the enemy and the good news is, that Jesus came to destroy the devil's work (1 John 3:8 c). Apostle Paul reminded the Ephesians Church of the living reality that they were facing on an ongoing basis in chapter 6 verse 12 *"For our struggle is not against flesh and blood, but against the rulers, against the authorities, against the powers of this dark world and against the spiritual forces of evil in the heavenly realms."*

"If we stand for nothing we will fall for anything", an expression challenging us to have a belief system in order to keep us going in a direction which are worth the effort. Isaiah puts it nicely in chapter 7:9 c *"If you do not stand firm in your faith, you will not stand at all."* For the Israelites in the Old Testament the laws, decrees and the commands of God handed down to them was the Godly divine standards for their lives to be build upon. Their adherence to the requirements of God would guarantee their success and prosperity in life. Deuteronomy 28:1-2 confirms it; *"If you fully obey the*

Lord your God and carefully follow all his commands I give today, the Lord your God will set you high above all the nations on earth. All these blessings will come upon you and accompany you if you obey the Lord your God..." Their disobedience would have the opposite effect which resulted in the wrath of God against their sins. Deuteronomy 28:15 says: "*However, if you do not obey the Lord you God and do not carefully follow all his commands and decrees I am giving you today, all these curses will come upon you and overtake you...*" Their obedience to the Word of God truly whether good or bad, reflected throughout their lives. Their kind of lives had a direct bearing on their application of the Word of God. Like us today the Israelites had the opportunity to choose between life and death, blessings and curses and the original intent of God with regards to them and us obeying His commands and decrees, were and are to come into a love relationship with Him. He wants us to be His people, and He wants to be our God. Oh how He wants to commune with us! Deuteronomy 30:19-20 says: "*This day I call heaven and earth as witnesses against you that I have set before you life and death, blessings and curses. Now choose life, so that you and your children may live and that you may love the Lord your God, listen to his voice, and hold fast to him. For the Lord is your life...*"

I believe what our people in our world need today in the light of decline in morality and increased corruption, is to return to God himself on the basis of faith in his word, through the working of his Holy Spirit. Repentance leads to Godly prosperity according to Deuteronomy chapter 30. We must adopt Biblical values, principles and beliefs and build our lives upon it. God desires jealously, to be number one in all of our lives as He created us in His likeness with a specific purpose and destiny according to Genesis 1: 27-28. David asked in Psalm 144:3 "O Lord, what is man that you care for him, the son of man that you think of him?" Our values, principles and beliefs determine our behaviour to a large extend and we need to adjust our values, principles and beliefs in order to change our behaviour. I believe that if we firmly established our values, beliefs and principles we are better of to build our behaviour accordingly and hence be better empowered to deal responsibly with perceptions in our relationship with people in general.

Chapter 9

You Are What You Digest

We do not always realise that our behaviour are influenced also amongst others, by external factors, the things we keep ourselves busy with. What you entertain yourself with like the kind of books you read, the kind of movies or programs you watch on television, the kind of friends you hang out with, the kind of church you attend ect makes us who we are. For example if you entertain your sexual appetite on a regular basis through pornographically material, the media and books you are feeding yourself in becoming a victim of its content and qualify yourself as a candidate to become involved in the practice of sexual immorality or you just making yourself dirty with its contents. For people to fall into the act of adultery is a calculated act which resulted as part of a process whereby people feeded themselves with the idea over a period of time. Just what you sow you reap! What you conditioned yourself to will evidently show forth in your behaviour and will eventually exposes a person.

We must not underestimate the power of conditioning and we can think of various examples of how habits, whether good or bad, get formed originally. How does a person becomes a alcoholic? There is the first drink which led to many and by the power of conditioning the person become addicted and end up in being an alcoholic. The same we can say about any form of drug addiction. It begin in a very innocent manner but by space repetition it becomes a deadly life threatened habit which are currently as I am writing this book destroying lives, families and communities. You are what you digest! The influences you expose yourselves to will have its workout in your life whether good or bad! The theme of this book is to make you realise that you got the power to choose to change to the better and so helping others also to say yes to change! I do not know you or do not know where you are, but the good news is you can change if you rightly decided too. We firstly need to acknowledge that we ought to change if we want to live a better life by increasing the quality thereof. My motto in life is: "The biggest room in the world is the room of improvement."

Surely ones input determines your output is a reality I discovered looking back in my career in the manufacturing concern. You got to determine your output or your objectives by engaging on the preset activities and adjustments along the road that would enable you to achieve your ultimate goals. We are so expose to all shorts of influences and I am of the opinion that we have to halt and assess what we are busy with and whether it is in line with our values, beliefs and principles. One thing about us as a person that tells a story on its own is the kind of friends we hang out with. Those we closely associated ourselves with tell a lot about who we are, because you are known by your friends. Doesn't the saying goes "birds of the feather flock together". Due to the dynamics involve in friendship, friends are strategically positioned to influence our lives tremendously. There are things like peer and group pressure and we must guard us against all negative influences which contradicts our values, beliefs and principles. We must stand up for it or fall for everything or anything!

Even the kind of books' content we read contribute to our personal data base which in turn determines our behaviour. We must realize the dynamics of what we choose to expose ourselves towards, as it does impact on our behaviour especially if it happens regularly over a period of time.

Chapter 10

Be Real

We are all unique individuals with different personality types and in our modern day and age, people are challenged to be real in their relationship with others. Some people prefer to live a private life as they are afraid to be rejected by others by showing themselves. As people have preconceived ideas of others that disallow or hinders growth in relationships. One of the biggest breakthroughs in relationships that we may have is the ability to be real by stopping all of our pretences and pulling down our masks, and be the real me, you and us we can ever be! That is the best point of departure from where we can make all possible adjustments along the path of building healthy relationships.

People for various reasons putting up masks, and consequently put up a big act in their dealings with other people. We all got choices on how we do want to project ourselves to the outside world, but I have come to the realization that in spite of all the hiding by some, there is an inside cry within us to show the world the real me. I'm certain that we do not desire to live a lie or a double life. To be able to handle unverified perception responsibly in a systematic manner to illuminates all possible misunderstandings or misconceptions, we ought to be real and original, maintaining a positive self image. When we live from our inner convictions, together with being conscious of our values, beliefs and principles and adhere thereto we are best set up to be real to ourselves and to the people around us. When we real we appreciate to be people of integrity, character, honesty, loyalty, commitment and just to be someone when nobody's sees.

We may hide things from mankind and at times seems to get away with our unrighteousness, but we will never be able to bypass God because He is an all knowing, all present and all mighty God. The Bible says in Hebrews 4:13 *"Nothing in all creation is hidden from God's sight. Everything is uncovered and laid bare before the eyes of him to whom we must give account."* Only the word of God got the power to expose us and showing the real us from where we can progress trusting God through the power of His Spirit to transform us. The verse preceding says: *"For the word of God . . . judges the thoughts and attitudes of the heart."* As people of the word of God we are obligated to allow God's word to have his way in and through our lives, changing and growing us from the one degree of glory to the next, as quoted before according to 2 Corinthians 3:18. One reason I think why we struggle to be real is due to the fact that we never learn to be real before God, out of reverential fear that is due unto Him. Only the blood of Christ, through cleansing us has the power to enable us to have a real relationship with God. Hebrews 9:14 says: *"How much more, then, will the blood of Christ, who through the eternal Spirit offered himself unblemished to God, cleanse our consciences from acts that lead to death, so that we may serve the living God!"*

We need to make inherently a decision to come forward and project the real us, embracing feedback from the outside world, and grow continuously from there. As I briefly addressed the issue of self image in chapter 4, we all need first of all to discover ourselves in terms of our values, beliefs and principles. We must choose to be real and live to the fullest and refuse to settles with second or third best. We owe it to ourselves to develop to our full potential which can only be done through active participation through a continuous personal developing attitude, that embrace change to the better in service of humanity.

Chapter 11

Leadership

As I said before, the complexity of the individual increases within a group situation and we all behave differently in various settings and circumstances. In our interaction with one another we displays our concept of leadership especially within conflict situations. The kind of leadership we being exposed are most likely to shape our manner of leadership. Taken the theories of leadership into account we have to redefine our understanding thereof. My experiences in the different disciplines I have been involved with, like marketing, sales, finance, production and human resources I came to the practical realization that leadership is all about influence. However, within Christ I came to believe in servant hood leadership. We lead by hearing, obeying, following and serving God and our fellow men. Jesus was chosen, mandated, confirmed and anointed to save humanity through his sacrificial atonement death at the cross of Calvary. Jesus' road to free us came about with many temptations, opposition, assaults, accusations, threads and suffering. In spite of all these amongst others he was dedicated, focussed and devoted to his mission, knowing the end from the start with one thing in mind at all times throughout his public ministry: Then I said, 'Here I am—it is written about me in the scroll—*I have come to do your will, O God.*' (Hebrews 10:7).

In accomplishing his mission Jesus operated in total obedience and submission to his Father and only desired to please Him. The gospel writer according to John says in chapter 17 verse 4 *"I have brought you glory on earth by completing the work you gave me to do."* In John 12:49 Jesus said: *"For I did not speak of my own accord, but the Father who sent me commanded me what to say and how to say it."* As the first missionary to planet earth Jesus was prepared to leave his place of glory and took on the form of a servant and became like us purposely so that we might become like him. The willingness to do the right thing at the right time in order to achieve a greater purpose to the benefit of millions of people's life, even to the point of death of himself tells me everything about the kind of leadership Jesus displayed. Our freedom from the bondage of sin was on His mind which kept him going on all the way to the cross, His ultimate victory over Satan of whom He made a public spectacle. On an occasion Jesus said He has come for the sick and needy and not for the righteous ones and that He came to serve and not to be served.

However, in our world today people in organisations, institutions and all workplaces tend to do everything in their power to get to the top competing for higher paid positions at the cost sometimes of relationship, moral and ethical values. People want to be better and more important than others regardless of how they climb the ladder of success. I believe that we must afford ourselves the opportunity to develop to our full potential so that we can add value to our society, and hence earn or generate our income to cover all our life expenses or just basically fulfil in all of our needs. I belief that the better we are equip with the required skills in all various fields of disciplines of career the more we ought to become servants of society at large. But the practical reality proofs to be different, that the more we climb the ladder of success the more puffed-up, proud and arrogant we become, which in turn negatively impact our efficiency in service delivery. The kind of leadership displayed by people in senior managerial positions of their organisations covers from abuse of authority to manipulation, instead of developing the leaders in their subordinates and allowing them to make mistakes in their development process. Their autocratic and dominating style of management reflect at times their concept of leadership. In essence I came across that they just exposes their weaknesses like insecurities, superiorities, lack of attention and love and their super shallow value systems. We must positively and strategically influence people's behaviour to the level that they achieve the desired results for which they are responsible and accountable for. We need to realize the awesome opportunity we have at times to contribute towards others increase performance competencies level, and we ought to seize the moments. Another secular definition of leadership e.g leadership is not positional, but functional is so true as we are constantly challenged to deliver the desirable outcomes.

My personal understanding about servant hood leadership is capture in the answer of Jesus to His disciples in their dispute about who is the greatest amongst them. Matthew 20: 25-28 says: 25 Jesus called them together and said, "You know that the rulers of the Gentiles lord it over them, and their high officials exercise authority over them. 26 Not so with you. Instead, *whoever wants to be great among you must be your servant*, 27 *and whoever wants to be first must be your slave—28 just as the Son of Man did not come to be served, but to serve, and to give his life as a ransom for many*." Our concept of leadership does impact the quality of our mannerism in interacting with other people. We need to try to understand others more than to try to be understood by others, thus serving the interest of others more.

Chapter 12

Work At Your Dreams

Many times we get stuck in the world of unverified perceptions and having frustrations in our dealings with people, just to find out that we are unfulfilled and not living our dreams. It is sad to realize that the millions of people are buried in our graveyards with untapped potential into eternity. There is nothing so worse than to be alive without a dream or a vision. Some translations reads Proverbs 29:18 as follow *"without a vision my people parish"* A dream is the gap between where you are currently in comparison where you want to be in future. Differently put, it is the gap between the current reality and the future reality of your life. There is a bridge to follow to arrive at our destination. This bridge consist of short, medium and long term goals to be set and achieve—a follow through realistic step by step plan necessary to follow to realized our dreams. It is not meant for us to be dreamers only, but people who live to their full potential have learned to put their dreams into actions in order to make it come true as it will not only happens—we must make it happen ourselves! Our dreams are just future realities and we just got to work at it to have it and embrace the new opportunities, and deals with the challenges that come along with it.

A fulfilled person tends to have lesser issues and is more empowered to engage properly and constructively in relationship building than a person with a lot of outstanding issues that needs to be dealt with. We can become what we dream to be and the only limitations we may have are those that we put upon ourselves. We box God, others and ourselves and we cannot get out of our cages breaking the walls of our limitations in pursuing our respective dreams. Dreams can come true and we got to believe it in order to achieve it. Our faith creates our realities. We are created with a Godly purpose to fulfil and we need to discover that by determining our desires, capabilities, skills or just what we want to become with everything that is within us. What would give us a kick imagining what we want to do from the bottom of our hearts? For what would you move mountains and valleys, and prepared to apply the necessary disciplines in order to become that which you would do for the rest of your life? What do you desire to do career wise which you would enjoy doing without realising that you are not working but living to the fullest. Wouldn't it be ideal to perform your duties you are passionate about?

From all my interdisciplinary exposure in various industries I have learned that people in general are occupying their second or third choice concerning their career, and in spite of excellent remunerations are not necessarily happy people. Fulfilments of dreams just not automatically happens or just arrive at you doorstep. We need to take ownership of the dreams inside us and actively follow through on a detailed action plan to take us through all the stages till we accomplish our objectives one by one. We must be prepared to do possible adjustments and sacrifices along the way as we may come across many variables which require our flexibility. We must become conscience of the reality that we are here on earth for a specific purpose and for a specific time, to make the world around us a better place and especially in our dealings with one another. Jesus is saying in the gospel according to John 10:10 "The thief comes only to steal and kill and destroy; *I have come that they may have life, and have it to the full.*"

We all got seeds of greatness inside us that screams to be develop just because we were being created into His image—we are wonderfully made and blessed! In Isaiah 66:9 the Lord says "*Do I bring to the moment of birth and not give delivery?*" Isaiah prophesied about the future overflowing abundance that awaited Israel at the time of this prophesy. Again the prophesy of Jeremiah 29:11 comes to light: "*For I know the plans I have for you, declares the Lord, plans to prosper you and not to harm you, plans to give you hope and a future.*" God requires our active participation through obedience unto Him that would release the ultimate blessings of Him upon our lives. God blessings upon our lives are a direct result of our obedience unto Him and in retrospect our disobedience unto Him would release His curses or wrath upon our lives. It is written in Jeremiah 7:23 "but I give them this command: *Obey me, and I will be your God and you will be my people. Walk in all the ways I command you, that it may go well with you.*" Obedience to God is my personal definition of successful living. Intimacy with God through Christ our Lord and Saviour is key to get at His heartbeat for our lives and to follow His dream for our lives. Believe in your dreams in order to step into the realization thereof and with faith in God all things are possible. Don't let anyone talk you out of your dreams for dreams can come true!

Chapter 13

It's Never Too Late

It is never too late to embark on a project, vision or dream for your life. As long as you got breath there is a purpose for living, even in the face of defeat. As long as we experience today we can hear His voice and obey Him. As long as it is today it is the day that the Lord has made and we must rejoice and be glad in it. It is also not over with us until God says it's over. He has the last and final say over our lives. God who holds and sustains the whole universe, He created Himself with the power of His own word. He is in control of life, the source and the giver thereof. We need to build our lives around Him and to please Him alone, and so fulfil the reason why we are created.

A lot of people are in a passive mode and very reluctant to do or try to do anything new in order to achieve something valuable and precious to them, but due to past failures, hurt and critique by some they are afraid to begin again. When we down and out and ashamed and afraid to get out of the valleys of despair, it is never too late to begin all over again. The God of the Bible is the God of beginnings who waits upon us to make of us winners regardless of our past failures and mistakes. Do not give up or quit as it is never too late to turn to Him for a brand new beginning or a total make over—never to be the same again! Many people on a very later stage of their lives realise the emptiness and become aware of a deep seated desire to pursue, for various reasons in majority cases are reluctant to give it a go. People had failed tremendously in the past and still suffer of the humiliation thereof that they just can begin or venture out to start with something new.

Some came through divorces or just bad relationship that speaks of abuse, mistreatment, manipulation, domination and suffers greatly that it appears that they would never be freed of the effects thereof. Others serve their sentences in jails and some are caught up in all of our various institutions because of various transgressions of the law and just bad influences that made them victims. Family abuse to suicidal acts in society not even to refer to the rape and crime rate, tells us a story of people who lost it in life who needs to know that they can all start all over again. Yes, they can begin again! God can change victims into victors! Acts 3:19-20 teach us hope for a fresh start: *"Repent, then, and turn to God, so that your sins may be wiped out, that times of refreshing may come from the Lord, and that he may send the Christ, who has been appointed for you—even Jesus,"* There is for the cruellest murderer, rapist, thieve, drug and wine smuggler hope in Christ for a new fresh new start, a new beginning, to undergo a brain and heart surgery never to be the same again. Jesus said about His own mission that He has come for the sick and the unrighteous for those in need—those who need the doctor. Regeneration, justification, sanctification and joy, peace and righteousness have come our way through the cross of Jesus Christ. Only God through Jesus Christ can put us right with Him on the basis of our faith in Him. 2 Corinthians 5:17 say it all: *"Therefore, if anyone is in Christ, he is a new creation; the old has gone, the new has come!"* It is not important what men says about us but what God thinks and say about us. His transforming power can take us from the deep muddy clay of society and put our feet on the rock that cannot be shaken—for His kingdom is an everlasting one. Matthew 11:12 speaks of the reality of the kingdom of God: "From the days of John the Baptist until now, *the kingdom of heaven has been forcefully advancing, and forceful men lay hold of it."*

A new beginning is only found in Him who created us into His image and who alone can transform our lives into His likeness with ever-increasing glory according to 2 Corinthians 3:18. We need to acknowledge that our lives are in a mess and that we need help to get out of it, by turning to Him in the light of Scripture for our salvation and redemption. He delights to make our life anew, over again. This process of beginning again affords us with so much confidence and restored dignity, which energises and empowers us to engage constructively in relationships in living a more fulfilled live. Only He can restore our fallen souls and stabilises our lives and provides us with new priorities and outlook on life, just to begin all over again for the Bible says in Acts 17:28 *"For in him we live and move and have our being."* When we move out in Him we grow in his love that enables us to even love our enemies from a sincere heart.

Listens to Isaiah 43:18-19 *"Forget the former things; do not dwell on the past. See, I am doing a new thing! Now it springs up; do you not perceive it? I am making a way in the desert and streams in the wasteland."*

Chapter 14

Men Pleaser Or God Pleaser

Man tends to live a life of stage performance and trying to impress or win the approval of others, at the cost of compromising his value, beliefs and principles. People go the extra mile just to be accepted by others. The lot of bribery and corruption in the political, business and religious arenas support the effort of people that serves the interest of others and themselves just to be in or cool, to accomplish their sense or need to be associated with. We bend ourselves at times to collect complements from others due to our insecurities and lack of a positive self image. In social circles we associate with those who give us the greatest feedback of approval and acceptance. We hang out with the "Jones" as it makes us look and feel good to be important in the eyes of people we value a lot. We surround those of influence, power and authority and will do anything just to be in their good books, just in case we need them in future. Relationships are many a time maintained just for what people can get something out of it. Surely I need to make this note that what I mentioned thus far in this chapter is not a generalisation, but some of the realities that does occur in relationships between people.

People become slaves of others whether they are manipulated or dominated by others or whether they seek the acceptance or approval of others. One thing I started to employ in my personal relationship with suppose close friends is, that I only engage on a continual personal basis with them if they are prepared too, to reach out to me and my family—it's a give and take for the growth of our friendship. Even in the world of employment people perform eye services to their bosses instead of being driven by their passion to perform to their job requirements and in the process adds value to their organisations. Employees need to take ownership of their responsibilities for which they are accountable for. We need to be task driven and execute it with the required skills to the best of our abilities. Our actual performances must earn the complements and the rewards of our bosses or employers. As believing employees we are encourage even to do better especially when our employers are fellow believers according to 1 Timothy 6: 2 "*Those who have believing masters are not to show less respect for them because they are brothers. Instead, they are to serve them even better, because those who benefit from their service are believers, and dear to them. These are the things you are to teach and urge on them.*"

We can be a great success in the eyes of the world and still be a great failure in the eyes of God. The same applies with the other way around—a great success in the eyes of God but greatly rejected or a failure in the eyes of the world. With regard to the chapter title we cannot have both in one world, and hence we got to choose whom we want to live for or want to please. The writer of the letter of Hebrews says in chapter 11 verse 6 "*And without faith it is impossible to please God . . .*" We are further warned in the first epistle of John chapter 2 from verse 15 to 17 as follows: "15 *Do not love the world or anything in the world. If anyone loves the world, the love of the Father is not in him.* 16 *For everything in the world—the cravings of sinful man, the lust of the eyes and the boasting of what he has and does—comes not from the Father but from the world.* 17 *The world and its desires pass away, but the man who does the will of God lives forever.*" We cannot serve God and mammon. The Bible says in Matthew 6:24 "*No one can serve two masters. Either he will hate the one and love the other, or he will be devoted to the one and despise the other. You cannot serve God and Money.*" I do urge and challenge you to be a God pleaser instead of a people pleaser. The Bible further informs us in the gospel of Mark 8:36 "*What good is it for a man to gain the whole world, yet forfeit his soul?*" To be a God pleaser means to deny self and to follow Christ. Luke 9:23-24 says "*Then he said to them all: if anyone would come after me, he must deny himself and take up his cross daily and follow me.* 24 *For whoever wants to save his life will lose it, but whoever loses his life for me will save it.*" It further states: " . . . *in the last days . . . people will be lovers of themselves . . . rather than lovers of God*" (2 Timothy 3:1, 2, 4).

God pleasers are people of integrity, character, sound Biblical values and codes of behaviour, which enables them to honesty and faithfully interact with other people in a dignified manner. Believers in Christ are just more resourceful to verify all possible perceptions by illuminating any misperceptions so that truth may at all times prevail.

Chapter 15

How To Treat Others

For me the world revolves around people and especially how we treat people in general. Our mannerism and way of treating others are truly a reflection of our perception of God revealed. If we can get only in the habit of doing role reversals it would help us a bit to understand the other party better. Our real inner man gets exposed in our thoughts, attitudes and actions towards others. Just from a human point of view it is world wide accepted as good practice to do to others what you want others to do to you. To treat others reasonable without prejudice or any form of discrimination without the violation of any rights is ideal.

But we need to assess and determine the current reality of how we treat others, to determine where we need to make any adjustment if necessary at all, as we are products of our past and are conditioned in our behavioural patterns. Sometimes we do realise that we ought to change but do not know how to change, and if not confronted by others we will never change. However, whenever we decide to change in the way we treat others it surely needs to start at the way we perceive them to be. We are at times blind in our judgments of others due to various reasons like preconceived ideas or just misperceptions, and we need to start to look afresh and in different ways at our fellow human beings.

I do suggest that the best place to look for answers like these is to go to God's manual for mankind, the Bible. The reason is simple because as God created humanity for a purpose and destiny how does He values mankind and how does He perceive mankind to be in his relationship towards Himself and towards others? To look to others through the eyes of "Jesus" is where biblically God wants us to be. He left His place in glory and took on the form of a servant and became like us so that He could freed us from the bondage of sin and death, and eternal separation from the presence of God. He became like us so that we might become like Him. This we do by embracing His transforming Word and let it dwells within us with all wisdom as we teach and admonish one another in all thankfulness towards Him (Colossians 3:16).

The moment we think of ourselves better than others is the day we rob ourselves of tremendous blessings, wealth and prosperity. It is only in our interpersonal relationship and effective communications that we discover ourselves in service to our fellowman. No one although uniquely created, is an island that can grow on its own. We desperately are in need of one another and hence is it important that we do improve in skills in terms of interpersonal relationships and communications. If we mistreat others by thinking of ourselves as better than them, proud and arrogant we limit our own growth potential and rob ourselves of unspeakable joy. If we belittle others by looking down on them because they do not match our criteria of status, and reckon that we've got it all, is the day we stopped living. A dead man is better than a man alive not realising his dependence upon God and others.

We need to restore one another's dignity, trust and respect by the manner we treat each other. No one is more important than the other, but we are all equally importantly created in the eyes of God, having an equal opportunity to be become unequal with reference to the degree we take ownership of developing ourselves (by acquiring all required and necessary skills) to our maximum potential. It is inevitable that in pursuing our dreams we got to treat others as part of the process of becoming a better develop person in service to society. We need to treat people in a way that would unleashes their God's given potential and contributing or fostering a culture of continuous change that would last and beneficial to the next generation. We would not only free others but ourselves in being better equipped and empowered to responsibly handle unverified perceptions, in building a better nation for tomorrow.

The adherence to the great commandments of God handed down through Moses to the Israelites, are of outmost importance as love does not harm our neighbours, thus the fulfilment of the Law. It is written according to Galatians 6:10 *"Therefore, as we have opportunity, let us do good to all people . . ."* 1 John 3:11 *"This is the message you heard from the beginning: We should love one another."* 1 John 3:18 *"Dear children, let us not love with words or tongue but with actions and in truth."* 1 John 4: 10 *"This is love: not that we loved God, but that he loved us and sent his Son as an atoning sacrifice for our sins. 11 Dear friends, since God so loved us, we also ought to love one another. 12 No one has ever seen God; but if we love one another, God lives in us and his love is made complete in us."*

Chapter 16

Social, Economic and Political Influences

The social, economical and political influences on our behaviour must never be underestimated or ignored. Concepts, ideologies, beliefs and cultures are powerful forces that can either unite or divide a nation. Societal structures that support these influences over a period of decades can be detrimental to the health, wealth and prosperity of a country. Proverbs 14:34 says: *"**Righteousness exalts a nation, but sin is a disgrace to any people.**"*

Within the context of the South African political background of white minority dominance over the majority since 1948 until the moment of our countries democracy in 1994, we all have been hurt in one way or another, through a political ideology of apartheid. Surely this manner of government set the tone socially and economically and hence today twenty years of democracy we can still see the discrepancies with regards to social and economical development between the various races of our country. Whites are still the have ones and are still strongly dominates the economy of South Africa. All of the current government initiatives on affirmative action and black economical empowerment are still not proven be successful as whites with their old mindsets in majority cases I came across for the past 27 years, are still ruling and reigning in workplaces determining with an old mindset how to bypass not to appoint rightly the previously disadvantage people in senior highly paid positions. The other side of the coin is also true that African blacks view it at times as a quick way to get to the top regardless whether they are the best fit qualified candidate for any given position. Education must path our ways to freedom in order to participate in the opportunities our beautiful country has to offer.

Everywhere it seems that whites adopted delaying tactics, trying to protect their heritage of the past as if it is possible in the presence of the writings against the wall. This phenomenon I see in model c schools, multicultural churches, the world of sports amongst others where whites hold tight to their controls afraid that they would loose by letting go and let South Africa be! How do one explains where a school for example comprises of learners in the majority other than whites, with a white dominant personnel and in some cases in the absence of anyone personnel with colour. How do one explains that in a multicultural church denomination the leadership are only whites whereby people of so call colour are allowed to aspire to a certain level of leadership determining by the whites. How do one explains that you got still the majority of companies in all of our various industries with the absence of people of so call colour in their top leadership in majority of instances? There are exceptions to the rule but the status quo are the current reality which in essence does not unites people but rather continuously enforcing an conditioned behaviour of an outdated unjust ideology. We all need to move together in a direction that enhances human relations and to improve a safe and secure society for us all. We are all co-responsible through our behaviour that stems from our value systems to create through our attitudes an atmosphere or environment that improves interaction and communication where we can care and share for one another. **WE ALL CAN CHOOSE TO CHANGE AND COME FREE** wherever we are in this world.

People other than whites in South Africa were degraded and robbed of opportunities to live their dreams in the country of their birth. They were denied access to the best educational institutes the country has to offer at the time and degraded and humiliated in not sharing in the wealth the country has to offer. They were belittled and looked down at by the ruling party at the time as lesser citizens of their respective countries. Their inferior houses, schools, roads, amongst other inferior public facilities at the time of apartheid and degree of lack of wealth possession in comparison with the whites, speaks a hurtful story itself. How could a minority political party been allowed to ruled for such a long period, only to find out years later since 1994 that they were wrong all the time. They were guilty of an unjust political system and consequently guilty of mistreating people unfairly and unjustly. They sin against humanity and insulted God who created us all into His image according to Genesis 1:27 and in the process has gathered the wrath of God against them—which led to the fall of the National Party in 1994.

The same applies to the current ANC government not to repeat the mistakes and sins of the past and being found guilty from a majority rule point of view, to sin against the people of our country by excluding the minorities to stop participating in the wellbeing of South Africa. The moment any government violate the ordinances, degrees, prescribes, values and principles of God according to Scripture they sin against God and against the people they serve. They also will fall if they fail to govern and serve the country as one people leading us all forth in a free for all society with equal opportunities for us all. History are facts and we can't play around the bush with what and why things happened in the past. We need to speak the truth to our children of today about our historical past and stop trying to live in denial or lying about it. They got the right to know the truth in order to embrace informed their hopeful future of prosperity to be shared with all fellow countrymen.

That's part of our past we all need to deal with in a manner that would free us all from the inside to the outside, never to be the same again! No race group are better off than the other but we all are dependent upon one another and need to embark on a cooperative, join, harmonious effort and demonstration to free one another from the bondage and effects of the devilish political system of apartheid that has and still have on the behaviour of the majority of South Africans. We must never underestimate the power of any political ruling party's ideology that is effecting and shaping the behaviour of a nation. It can either divide or unite a nation! We as South Africans have been torn apart from one another as fellow human beings on the basis of men's ideas which are in direct violation with God's greatest commandments to us as written in Mark 12:30 *"Love the Lord your God with all your heart and with all your mind and with all your strength. 31 The second is this: Love your neighbour as yourself. There is no commandment greater than these."* We need to help one another to unpack the baggages of the past and to heal the broken hearted, setting one another free as we embrace the love of God in Christ poured out into our lives by means of the Holy Spirit, in letting go and to let God! Only God can empowers us to break the barriers of injustice, prejudice, racial discrimination, oppression, domination, manipulation, intimidation, indoctrination, pride, arrogance, superiorities, inferiorities, fear, humiliation amongst others. Only the love of God has the power to truly unite us under Himself in Christ Jesus. 1 John 4:18 *"There is no fear in love. But perfect love drives out fear, because fear has to do with punishment. The one who fears is not made perfect in love. 19 We love because he first loved us. 20 If anyone says, I love God, yet hates his brother, he is a liar. For anyone who does not love his brother, whom he has seen, cannot love God, whom he has not seen. 21 And he has given us this command: Whoever loves God must also love his brother."*

God's invitation through the gospel of Jesus Christ to us, is to engage us in a personal relationship with Him, are extended to all nations, creed and culture of all times, since the fall of men. We can come through and be on top and healthy in our interracial, cross-cultural relationship and live in peace with all men if we so willingly choose to change and adhere to Biblical solutions in dealing with any issue of conflict. We can free ourselves, our families and children and friends and even our communities if we choose to change and come to the open, to his light, himself and forgive others for the wrong they has done towards us or what we has done to them. It is a simple matter of forgiving others, by letting them free, by speaking them free and letting them go and releasing ourselves from the bondage of unforgiveness and bitterness and bad memory. In James 5: 16 it is written; *"Therefore confess your sins to each other and pray for each other so that you may be healed. The prayer of a righteous man is powerful and effective."*

It is imperative that we meet each other at the feet of the cross of Jesus Christ and first and foremost experiences His pardon, forgiveness over our personal sins, so that we out of a Godly forgiveness-experience can forgive one another. Reconciliation and restoration can only be found through the value and essence of the cross of Jesus Christ. The cross signifies hope, new beginning, healing, restoration, forgiveness, peace, acceptance and most of all the unconditional love of God displayed to save humanity! The way of the cross is Gods manner of dealing with our healing from the bondage of sin and death! God in Jesus Christ reconciled the world unto Himself and according to 2 Corinthians 5:18-21 not counting our sins against us and entrusted to us the ministry of reconciliation. Through this demand he appeals through us all to all mankind to be reconciled with him in order that we all can become in Christ the righteousness of God.

CHOOSE TO CHANGE IN JESUS NAME!

Remember for the believers of our Lord, Saviour and King our battle is Biblical defined according to:

Ephesians 6:12 *"For our struggle is not against flesh and blood, but against the rulers, against the authorities, against the powers of this dark world and against the spiritual forces of evil in the heavenly realms."*

We can take courage in the fact that Jesus made of Satan a public spectacle and had overcome him at the cross of Calvary:

Colossians 2:15 *"And having disarmed the powers and authorities, he made a public spectacle of them, triumphing over them by the cross."*

The way forward till the bridegroom will return for the blemish bride, we the church need to enforce the victory of Christ at the cross of Calvary by faith in God through Christ Jesus:

Zechariah 4: 6(b) *"Not by might nor by power, but by my Spirit, says the Lord Almighty."*

CHOOSE TO CHANGE IN JESUS NAME!

Conclusion

We are living in a world of constant change and are pressurize to change with regards to our response to all the various information we are exposed to. From a consumer point of view we have increased options to choose between all the different products on the market that serves the same purposes at the end, and we have to decide on the best possible option that best suits our needs and situations. We got the power to choose to change or to become stagnant, and be irrelevant applicable in times when changes are inevitable and absolutely necessary. Sometimes we want to change the world and everyone around us, without realising that it is us that got to change to the good in order to add value to the lives of those we come in contact with. Real permanent change and transformation are only found in repentance and obedience to God. I firmly beliefs that God desire to work afresh through the person of the Holy Spirit, in the now where we are at, and to take us where he want us to be. We need to position ourselves in our relationship towards God, align ourselves with his word, and get his holy order in our lives so that we can be a living sacrifice offering ourselves to him (Romans 12:1).

God's intent through his holy word is to make our lives a dwelling place of his presence through faith in Christ, and through the working of the Holy Spirit. One of my greatest focuses is to live a life more controlled by the Holy Spirit. Men just after the fall at the beginning of Genesis were ever since called men back by God unto himself according to Genesis 3:9. The last book of the Bible provides us with the demonstration of a loving God knocking at the door of each individual to be restored unto himself, according to Revelation 3:20. Intimacy with God is key, vital and of outmost importance! That's the best place to be of security, stability, growth and prosperity! We use to sing a song: "Friendship with Jesus fellowship divine, o what blessed sweet communion, Jesus is a friend of mine!"

2 Chronicles 7:14 says: *"if my people, who are called by my name, will humble themselves and pray and seek my face and turn from their wicked ways, then will I hear from heaven and will forgive their sin and will heal their land."*

Acts 3:19 *"Change (Repent) your mind (turn to God), so that your sins may be wiped (forgiven) out, that times of refreshing may come from (the presence of) the Lord."*

2 Corinthians 3:16 "But *whenever anyone turns to the Lord, the veil is taken away. 17 Now the Lord is the Spirit, and where the Spirit of the Lord is, there is freedom. 18 And we, who with unveiled faces all reflect the Lord's glory, are being transformed into his likeness with ever-increasing glory, which comes from the Lord, who is the Spirit."*

CHOOSE TO CHANGE IN JESUS NAME!